P9-CRB-899

Irlene Scott

To

(Linda Pyles Family

From

3-20-07   Feb 12-2007
                                    (80)

Date

Prayer-Letters to Heaven and God's Refreshing Response

Heavenly mail

Philis Boultinghouse

words of *love* from God

HOWARD
PUBLISHING CO.

Our purpose at Howard Publishing is to:

- *Increase faith* in the hearts of growing Christians
- *Inspire holiness* in the lives of believers
- *Instill hope* in the hearts of struggling people everywhere

Because He's coming again!

Heavenly Mail—Words of Love from God © 2002 by Philis Boultinghouse
All rights reserved. Printed in Mexico
Published by Howard Publishing Co., Inc.
3117 North 7th Street, West Monroe, Louisiana 71291-2227

02 03 04 05 06 07 08 09 10 11   10 9 8 7 6 5 4 3 2

Interior design by Steve Diggs
Edited by Jennifer Stair

1-58229-234-5

No part of this publication may be reproduced in any form without the prior written permission of the publisher except in the case of brief quotations within critical articles and reviews.

Unless otherwise noted, Scripture quotations are from the Holy Bible, New International Version. Copyright © 1973, 1978, 1984 by International Bible Society. Used by permission of Zondervan Bible Publishers. All rights reserved. Scripture quotations marked NLT are taken from the Holy Bible, New Living Translation, copyright © 1996. Used by permission of Tyndale House Publishers, Inc., Wheaton, Illinois 60189. All rights reserved. Scripture quotations marked NKJV are taken from the Holy Bible, New King James Version, © 1982 by Thomas Nelson, Inc.

I love the LORD because he hears and answers my prayers.

Because he bends down and listens,

I will pray as long as I have breath!

Psalm 116:1–2 NLT

Contents

A Word to the Reader

Writing a letter is a special way to express yourself to someone you care for. It allows you to convey your feelings, thoughts, and emotions in a way unlike any other.

And what about receiving mail in return? Who doesn't enjoy the feeling of going to the mailbox, opening the door, and finding that you've got mail? With anticipation, you open the envelope and read the words of a cherished loved one or a faraway friend. Even though the writer is not present, you feel the warmth that the two of you share, and your hearts are united once again. That's what happens when you read *Heavenly Mail: Words of Love from God*.

This unique book is filled with letters between someone like yourself and the very best Friend of all—your heavenly Father. You'll quickly identify with the prayers, written as letters to a loving God, because they convey the needs, emotions, feelings, and struggles that life presents on a regular basis. In heaven's response, you'll read personalized, paraphrased scriptures, also written as letters, and you'll experience the assuring presence and loving warmth that only heaven can give.

The love that fills these heavenly letters will remain with you, inspire you, and fill you with hope. Let this little book bring you closer to heaven and to words of love that will impact your todays, tomorrows, and the rest of your life.

A LETTER TO *Heaven*

Dear God in Heaven,

I come to You with mixed emotions. I know in my head that You love me—I've read of Your love in the Bible; I've heard it preached in church; I've even felt it at times. But do You love me *all* the time? I don't really see how You could.

I mean, there are times when I feel as if I have it together—when my life is in balance, when I've been kind to my family and coworkers, when I'm having successes at work—and I can see how You might love me then. But there are other times when I have absolutely *nothing* together.

I'm living through one of those times right now. My relationship with my spouse is filled with tension, I've been snapping at my children all week, and I'm in a real slump at work. And the scary part of it is, I've lost confidence in my ability to make things right again.

Somewhere inside me, I know that this distance I feel from You is a lack of trust in the power of Your love, but I can't seem to shake this feeling of separation from You.

I've got to know. I need to hear from You. Do You love me even now?

Your Unlovable Child

A LETTER FROM *Heaven*

Dear Beloved,

My love for you is not dependent on how you feel or what you've done. While I am a God who expects you to strive to please Me, I know that you are frail—that you are made only of dust. I know all about you: your weaknesses, your failings, your regrets, your doubts. I know these things, for I have created you.

I know your thoughts before you think them; I know exactly what you are going to say before you open your mouth. I know the good and the bad of you, and yet I love you still. I love you because that is what I do—it is My very essence. My love is not based on your performance. It is Who I am.

My love is unlike any earthly love you have known. For My love *never* fails. It is as vast as the heavens; it reaches beyond the clouds; it fills the entire earth. Though the mountains be shaken and the hills removed, yet My unfailing love for you will not be shaken. For I am a God who has compassion on you.

You ask if I love you even now. Yes, a thousand times over. Yes! I love you even now.

Your God of Everlasting Love

from 2 Peter 3:14; Psalms 103:14 NLT; 139:2–4
1 John 4:8; Psalms 36:5 NLT; 33:5 NLT; Isaiah 54:10

God's Word OF LOVE

1 JOHN 4:8
God is love.

DEUTERONOMY 7:9
Know therefore that the LORD your God is God; he is the faithful God, keeping his covenant of love to a thousand generations of those who love him and keep his commands.

PSALM 36:5 NLT
Your unfailing love, O LORD, is as vast as the heavens; your faithfulness reaches beyond the clouds.

PSALM 139:2–4
You perceive my thoughts from afar. You discern my going out and my lying down; you are familiar with all my ways. Before a word is on my tongue you know it completely, O LORD.

ISAIAH 54:10
"Though the mountains be shaken and
the hills be removed, yet my unfailing
love for you will not be shaken nor my
covenant of peace be removed," says the
LORD, who has compassion on you.

2 PETER 3:14
Make every effort to be found
spotless, blameless and at
peace with him.

PSALM 103:14 NLT
He understands how weak we are; he knows we are only dust.

A LETTER TO *Heaven*

Dear God of Direction,

I'm in need of a little direction. Well, that's really an understatement. I'm in need of a lot of direction. I've been trying to direct my own steps, and it's just not working. I'm one of those people who tries to do things myself, who thinks I don't need anyone else's help. And now, that kind of thinking has gotten me into a real mess.

In one way or another, every aspect of my life is out of control. I know it's because I have tried to map out my life without consulting You. I have allowed myself to be duped by Satan into following after this world's definitions of success and fulfillment. I have not sought Your guidance, and though it's hard to admit this, I didn't really want Your advice. I didn't want Your interference. I knew that walking in the confines of Your path would mean that some things in my life would have to change—and I didn't want to change.

Now, Father, I come to You, broken and humbled by what life on my own has done to me. I beg You now for what I've thus far spurned: Your guidance and direction. Please forgive me for shutting You out and ignoring Your teachings. Please interfere in me.

Your Unruly Child

A Letter from *Heaven*

Dear Unruly Child,

I've had My eye on you all along, waiting for you to turn to Me for help. It is no wonder that your life is out of control. You do not have the ability to direct your own steps, for your life is not your own.

If you will allow Me, I will instruct you and teach you in the way you should go. I will counsel and watch over you. I will guide you along the best pathway for your life.

As you yield your will to Mine, you will discover two eternal truths: If you will humbly submit to Me, in due time, I will lift you up. And if you will resist Satan and his hold on you, he will turn tail and run!

And as you look to Me for direction and acknowledge Me in all your ways, I will make your path level and your way smooth. I will guide you in the way of wisdom and lead you along straight paths. When you walk, your steps will not be hampered; when you run, you will not stumble. When the pathway before you is unfamiliar, I will turn the darkness into light. I will never forsake you.

You may be surprised to find that My path is not an unpleasant one. In fact, it is in My path that you will find true delight. When you stay within the confines of My commands, you will learn to run with abandon, for I will set your heart free.

Yes, My child, I will gladly interfere in you.

Your Faithful Guide

from Jeremiah 10:23; Psalm 32:8; 1 Peter 5:6
James 4:10, 7; Isaiah 26:7; Proverbs 3:6; 4:11–12
Isaiah 42:16; Psalm 119:35, 32

# *God's Word* OF LOVE

JEREMIAH 10:23
I know, O LORD, that a man's life is not his
own; it is not for man to direct his steps.

PSALM 32:8
I will instruct you and teach you
in the way you should go; I will
counsel you and watch over you.

JAMES 4:10
Humble yourselves before the
Lord, and he will lift you up.

JAMES 4:7
Submit yourselves, then, to God. Resist the
devil, and he will flee from you.

ISAIAH 26:7
The path of the righteous is level; O upright One,
you make the way of the righteous smooth.

PSALM 119:35
Direct me in the path
of your commands, for
there I find delight.

PSALM 119:32
I run in the path of your commands,
for you have set my heart free.

ISAIAH 42:16
I will lead the blind by ways they have
not known, along unfamiliar paths I will
guide them; I will turn the darkness
into light before them and make the
rough places smooth. These are the
things I will do; I will not forsake them.

PROVERBS 4:11–12
I guide you in the way of wisdom and lead you along
straight paths. When you walk, your steps will not be
hampered; when you run, you will not stumble.

A LETTER TO *Heaven*

Dear God,

I've been wronged, Lord, really wronged. Someone I trusted has betrayed me. She shared secrets of my heart that were not hers to share. I opened myself up to her, revealing things I'd never shared with another soul, and now I've found that my innermost feelings and pain have become the subject of casual conversation.

What am I to do with these feelings of anger and resentment? How do I get past them to the forgiving heart I know You want me to have. Right now, forgiveness seems as impossible as gathering the tale she has scattered. Besides the *difficulty* of forgiveness, I don't *want* to forgive her. My inclination is to distribute secrets she's shared with me—and believe me, I have some I could hurt her with.

Lord, I know You don't want me to seek revenge, and I know You don't want me to hold this anger in my heart. But I can think of little else besides the damage she's inflicted. And to make matters worse, she seems oblivious to the pain she's caused me or the wrong of her actions. How can I possibly forgive a person who isn't even sorry?

Do You really expect that of me?

Your Betrayed Child

A LETTER FROM *Heaven*

Dear Betrayed Child,

Believe Me when I say that I understand exactly how you feel. When I tell you what you need to do, know that I speak from experience.

I, too, have suffered betrayal, but at an infinitely greater level than you have or ever will endure. I have loved with a perfect love yet have been continually and severely rejected. If I kept a record of the sins against Me, no one—absolutely no one—would be able to stand before Me. But I am a merciful and forgiving God, even toward those who have rebelled against Me, and I do not let the actions of others determine My reaction. And neither should you.

Forgiveness, my child, is a matter of perspective. The wrong your friend committed against you pales in comparison to the wrongs you've committed against Me. Your forgiveness of others is intrinsically linked with your own forgiveness. For if you forgive others when they sin against you, I will forgive you.

And the answer to your question is *yes*. Yes, I do expect you to forgive your friend even if she does not express sorrow for her actions. Forgiveness is the way of love. It was the way of Jesus as He hung on the cross at the hands of evil men. Even of them, He said to Me, "Father, forgive them, for they don't know what they are doing."

Say with Me, "I will forgive her and remember her sins no more."

Your God of Forgiveness

from Psalm 130:3–4; Daniel 9:9; Matthew 18:23–35
Luke 6:37; Matthew 6:14–15; Luke 23:34
Jeremiah 31:34

God's Word OF LOVE

LUKE 23:34
Jesus said, "Father, forgive them, for they
do not know what they are doing."

JEREMIAH 31:34
I will forgive their wickedness and will
remember their sins no more.

PSALM 130:3–4
If you, O LORD, kept a record of sins, O Lord, who
could stand? But with you there is forgiveness.

DANIEL 9:9
The Lord our God is merciful and forgiving,
even though we have rebelled against him.

LUKE 17:4
If he sins against you seven
times in a day, and seven times
comes back to you and says, "I
repent," forgive him.

LUKE 6:37
Do not judge, and you
will not be judged. Do
not condemn, and you
will not be condemned.
Forgive, and you will
be forgiven.

MATTHEW 6:14–15
If you forgive men when they sin against
you, your heavenly Father will also forgive
you. But if you do not forgive men their sins,
your Father will not forgive your sins.

A LETTER TO *Heaven*

Dear God and Friend,

Dare I ask, O God, dare I hope that I could share with You the intimate relationship of *friend?* Is it possible, Sovereign Lord, that Your love for me could transcend the barriers of servant-Lord, of slave-Master? I *crave* a deeper relationship with You. I earnestly seek You; my soul thirsts for You. My heart and my flesh cry out for You. Like a deer pants for streams of water, so my soul pants for You.

You already know all about me; I want to know more about You. I want to know You in the way a friend would know You. I want my heart to be in tune with Yours. I want to know what brings You joy, what breaks Your heart, what about us You love, what offends You. I want to know *You.*

And Father, dare I ask even more? Can we be friends in a way that You derive joy from *me?* Can I share with You in Your pain? Can I care with You about matters of concern to You?

I know I'm not worthy to be Your friend, but then, I'm not worthy to be Your child, and You've adopted me as such. So maybe...

The thought of being Your friend is too big for me; my mind barely comes to the edges of the thought. But I'm trying to grasp the idea, and I want to pursue the possibility. Please expand my mind and my heart to make room for You.

Wanting More of You

portions from Psalms 42:1; 63:1; 84:2

A LETTER FROM *Heaven*

Dear Child and Friend,

Your request is not a small one, and fulfilling your request will be largely up to you. The pathway to friendship with Me is not an easy one, for to be close to Me, you must deny all of you. You must completely die to yourself and allow My Son to live in your place.

I *love* you no matter what you do, but friendship is a different matter. Friendship with Me is based on your obedience. You are My friend if you do what I command. If you obey Me, I will come to you and make My home with you. And as you grow in obedience, you will discover that My commands are not burdensome.

When Jesus left the glory of heaven, took on flesh, and actually lived among you, He opened the door to intimacy with Himself and with Me. You *can* know Me, and know Me intimately. The way to knowing Me is through My Son. If you know Him, you most certainly know Me.

I invite you to approach My throne of grace boldly and with confidence, knowing that I will extend My mercy and grace whenever you need it. You can come right into My presence, trusting completely in Me, for your heart has been sprinkled with My Son's blood. As you come close to Me, I will come close to you.

Your Eternal Friend

from Matthew 16:24 NKJV; Mark 8:34; Galatians 2:20
John 15:14–15; 14:15, 23–24; 15:10; 1 John 5:3
John 1:14; 14:7; Hebrews 4:16; 10:22; James 4:8

God's Word OF LOVE

MATTHEW 16:24 NKJV

Jesus said to His disciples, "If anyone desires to come after Me, let him deny himself, and take up his cross, and follow Me."

JOHN 15:14

You are my friends if you do what I command.

JOHN 14:23

Jesus replied, "If anyone loves me, he will obey my teaching. My Father will love him, and we will come to him and make our home with him."

JOHN 15:15

I no longer call you servants, because a servant does not know his master's business. Instead, I have called you friends, for everything that I learned from my Father I have made known to you.

1 JOHN 5:3

This is love for God: to obey his commands.
And his commands are not burdensome.

JAMES 4:8

Come near to God and he will
come near to you. Wash your
hands, you sinners, and purify
your hearts, you double-minded.

HEBREWS 4:16

Let us then approach the throne of
grace with confidence, so that we
may receive mercy and find grace
to help us in our time of need.

HEBREWS 10:22

Let us draw near to God with a sincere heart in
full assurance of faith, having our hearts sprinkled
to cleanse us from a guilty conscience and having
our bodies washed with pure water.

A LETTER TO *Heaven*

Dear God of the Living,

I've just come from another funeral, Lord, and I am sick to death of death! I know it is not of Your making, Lord, and I'm not complaining to You; I'm just so frustrated and mad that Satan has brought death into this world. You are the only one I can turn to. You alone offer peace.

I'll not bring You questions of *why?* I know why. We live in a broken world—a world not intended for eternal living.

But the pain. I hate the pain. The pain on the faces of the mom and dad who lost their only child at the age of eighteen. The agony in the heart of the young wife who will now raise four children alone. The creeping fear of the husband who just lost his wife and best friend of twenty-three years.

What are we all to do with the pain? How can we live joyfully in this world, knowing that those we love will leave us or that we will leave them?

I'm hurting, Lord. We're all hurting. I need a word from You. I need to feel Your touch. I need to be reminded in my heart of what I know in my head.

Your Hurting Child

A LETTER FROM *Heaven*

Dear Hurting Child,

You can cast all your anxieties on Me, for I care for you. Though you grieve now, I will turn your mourning into dancing; I will clothe you with joy.

I love you so much that I sent My one and only Son to die in your place so that after this life, you can live eternally with Me. Because of your faith, your grief is not like those who have no hope. For you know that Jesus died and rose again and that I will raise those who have fallen asleep in Him. And you also know that on that Last Day, I will send Jesus from heaven to gather all who belong to Me. First, the dead in Christ will rise—those whose leaving caused so much pain there on earth—then, the living believers will be caught up in the air with Him.

Knowing this, your heart can be glad and your mouth can rejoice, for I will not abandon any of My children to the grave. I will fill you with joy in My presence, with eternal pleasures at My hand.

Though death stings loved ones left behind, it has no victory over those who believe in Me. For in a flash—in the twinkling of an eye—you will all be changed. The perishable will put on the imperishable and the mortal will put on immortality. Knowing this, My child, you must stand firm and let nothing move you.

Your Eternal God

from 1 Peter 5:7; Psalm 30:11; John 3:16
1 Thessalonians 4:13–17; Psalm 16:8–11
1 Corinthians 15:51–52, 54–58

God's Word OF LOVE

1 PETER 5:7
Cast all your anxiety on him because he cares for you.

JOHN 3:16
For God so loved the world that he gave his one and only Son, that whoever believes in him shall not perish but have eternal life.

1 THESSALONIANS 4:13–17
Brothers, we do not want you to be ignorant about those who fall asleep, or to grieve like the rest of men, who have no hope. We believe that Jesus died and rose again and so we believe that God will bring with Jesus those who have fallen asleep in him. According to the Lord's own word, we tell you that we who are still alive, who are left till the coming of the Lord, will certainly not precede those who have fallen asleep. For the Lord himself will come down from heaven, with a loud command, with the voice of the archangel and with the trumpet call of God, and the dead in Christ will rise first. After that, we who are still alive and are left will be caught up together with them in the clouds to meet the Lord in the air. And so we will be with the Lord forever.

PSALM 16:8–11

I have set the LORD always before me. Because he is at my right hand, I will not be shaken. Therefore my heart is glad and my tongue rejoices; my body also will rest secure, because you will not abandon me to the grave, nor will you let your Holy One see decay. You have made known to me the path of life; you will fill me with joy in your presence, with eternal pleasures at your right hand.

PSALM 30:11

You turned my wailing into dancing; you removed my sackcloth and clothed me with joy.

1 CORINTHIANS 15:51–52, 54–58

Listen, I tell you a mystery: We will not all sleep, but we will all be changed—in a flash, in the twinkling of an eye.... When the perishable has been clothed with the imperishable, and the mortal with immortality, then the saying that is written will come true: "Death has been swallowed up in victory." "Where, O death, is your victory? Where, O death, is your sting?" The sting of death is sin, and the power of sin is the law. But thanks be to God! He gives us the victory through our Lord Jesus Christ. Therefore, my dear brothers, stand firm. Let nothing move you.

A LETTER TO *Heaven*

Dear God of Prayer,

Lately, it seems that my prayers are not going any farther than the ceiling of my house. I pray to You, asking for Your help, seeking Your wisdom, but I feel as if I'm talking to an empty chair. Do You hear me, Lord? Do You care about my problems? Do You truly intend to give me the desires of my heart?

It seems as if You have forgotten me—almost as if You've hidden Your face from me. I don't mean to be disrespectful, but how long must I wait to hear from You? Every morning I come to You with my request, and I wait expectantly to hear from You. Your Word tells me that if I will delight myself in You, if I will commit my ways to You and trust You, that You will give me the desires of my heart. But it's not happening, Lord.

In my distress, I have sought You. I prayed all night, with my hands lifted toward heaven, pleading with You to answer me. I can have no joy in my life until You act on my behalf. Have You rejected me? Is Your unfailing love gone? Have You forgotten to be kind? Has the door of Your compassion slammed shut?

But then I think of all the good You have done for me and others in the past. I know You are listening, Lord. I just need some reassurance.

Your Uncertain Child

*portions from Psalms 13:1; 119:84; 5:3
37:4–6; 77:2, 7, 9, 11*

A *Letter from Heaven*

Dear Uncertain Child,

You do well to remember all that I have done for you and others. Meditate on My works and consider My mighty deeds. For My ways are holy. I am the God who performs miracles, who displays My power among people. You can know with certainty that I am not ignoring your prayer and that I have not withdrawn My unfailing love from you. I love you so much that I bend down to listen to you.

I am close to all who sincerely call on Me. I fulfill the desires of those who fear Me; I hear your cries for help, and I will rescue you. You can be absolutely confident that I will listen to you whenever you ask for anything that lines up with My will. And you can know that if I am listening to your request, that I will surely give you what you've asked for.

Sometimes the reason you don't get what you desire is that you haven't asked Me. And at other times, you may ask and not receive because you've asked with wrong motives—planning to spend what you get on your own pleasures. But much of the time, it's just a matter of waiting on Me and trusting that I love you and will work all things together for your good.

You can call on Me anytime and know that I hear and care for you. Of this you can be certain.

Your Trustworthy God

from Psalms 77:11–14; 66:20 NLT; 116:1–2 NLT
145:18–19 NLT; 1 John 5:14–15 NLT; James 4:2–3
Psalms 27:14; 37:7; Proverbs 3:5; Romans 8:28 NLT

God's Word OF LOVE

PSALM 116:1–2 NLT
I love the LORD because he hears and answers my prayers. Because he bends down and listens, I will pray as long as I have breath!

PSALM 66:20 NLT
Praise God, who did not ignore my prayer and did not withdraw his unfailing love from me.

PSALM 77:11–14
I will remember the deeds of the LORD; yes, I will remember your miracles of long ago. I will meditate on all your works and consider all your mighty deeds. Your ways, O God, are holy. What god is so great as our God? You are the God who performs miracles; you display your power among the peoples.

PSALM 145:18–19 NLT
The LORD is close to all who call on him, yes, to all who call on him sincerely. He fulfills the desires of those who fear him; he hears their cries for help and rescues them.

ROMANS 8:28 NLT
God causes everything to work together for the good of those who love God and are called according to his purpose for them.

PSALM 27:14
Wait for the LORD; be strong and take heart and wait for the LORD.

PROVERBS 3:5
Trust in the LORD with all your heart and lean not on your own understanding.

1 JOHN 5:14–15 NLT
We can be confident that he will listen to us whenever we ask him for anything in line with his will. And if we know he is listening when we make our requests, we can be sure that he will give us what we ask for.

A LETTER TO Heaven

Dear God of Wisdom,

I need the wisdom of Your love, Lord. A friend of mine—a very dear friend—is in a real slump and is treating everyone around her badly—everyone: her family, her coworkers, her friends...me.

I see the pain in her eyes, and I know that the pain is the reason for her grumpy, unkind exterior. I also know her heart, Lord, and I know that at its center is a deep, abiding love for You and a desire to please You. But she seems oblivious to the pain she's causing others by her gruff, detached demeanor.

My quandary is this: Should I confront her about her behavior and try to get her to open up about her pain or simply ignore her actions and give her more time to work through her torment? My own feelings about the situation fluctuate. Sometimes I'm just flat mad at her and want her to grow up and get over it; at other times, my heart breaks for her and I know that "getting over it" is not as easy as snapping my fingers.

Help me, Lord. Give me wisdom to know how to deal with my friend's behavior. Supply me with insight into the best approach. I await Your guidance.

Your Child

A *L*ETTER FROM *Heaven*

Dear Child of Mine,

It is good that you seek My wisdom on this. The one overriding factor in deciding how to react to your friend is *love*. Responding out of love means not reacting out of your feelings of frustration and anger. But that doesn't mean that passivity is always the best approach. Sometimes confrontation is necessary. It's love that helps you decide.

Do not approach your friend out of selfish ambition or vanity, but instead, consider your friend's needs over your own. Let your attitude be that of Christ Jesus'. Before you address your friend, make sure that you are clothed with My characteristics: compassion, kindness, humility, gentleness, and patience.

It may be that you need to confront your friend. But if you do, do it for *her* good, not just to get your frustration off your chest. And if you have to speak a difficult truth, do it in love. Remember, it is your obligation to bear with your friend and forgive whatever grievances you may have against her—just as your heavenly Father has forgiven you. Whatever your approach, love your friend deeply—because love covers a multitude of sins.

Your God of Loving Confrontation

from 1 Corinthians 16:14; Philippians 2:3–5
Colossians 3:12; Romans 15:1–2; Ephesians 4:15
Colossians 3:13; Ephesians 4:2; 1 Peter 4:8

God's Word OF LOVE

1 CORINTHIANS 16:14
Do everything in love.

PHILIPPIANS 2:3–5
Do nothing out of selfish ambition or vain conceit, but in humility consider others better than yourselves. Each of you should look not only to your own interests, but also to the interests of others. Your attitude should be the same as that of Christ Jesus.

ROMANS 15:1–2
We who are strong ought to bear with the failings of the weak and not to please ourselves. Each of us should please his neighbor for his good, to build him up.

COLOSSIANS 3:12
Therefore, as God's chosen people, holy and dearly loved, clothe yourselves with compassion, kindness, humility, gentleness and patience.

EPHESIANS 4:15
Speaking the truth in love, we will in all things
grow up into him who is the Head, that is, Christ.

1 PETER 4:8
Above all, love each
other deeply, because
love covers over a
multitude of sins.

EPHESIANS 4:2
Be completely humble
and gentle; be patient,
bearing with one
another in love.

COLOSSIANS 3:13
Bear with each other and forgive whatever grievances you may
have against one another. Forgive as the Lord forgave you.

A LETTER TO *Heaven*

Dear God,

My heart is in shreds. I've lost someone very close to me, and I don't know if I can hold up under the pain. I know You've promised that You won't give us more than we can handle, but I think this might be over my limit. Life without this dear one is more than I can bear.

And the pain is more than emotional—it's physical. It feels as if an elephant was dropped onto my chest. It hurts; it's suffocating; it won't go away...

How am I to survive? How am I to live without this one I've loved for so long? Some have tried to comfort me, but no words have eased my pain. Others are telling me it's time I get on with my life, but my life now has a huge gaping hole. My life is not what it was, so how can I get on with it?

I can't seem to get anything accomplished. Some days I can't even drag myself out of bed, and on days that I do, my mind is in such a fog that I can't function.

I think I'm broken, Lord. Will I ever be whole again? Will I ever feel content and at peace?

Help me, God. It hurts so badly.

Your Broken Child

portions from 1 Corinthians 10:13

A LETTER FROM *Heaven*

Dear Broken Child,

Come to Me, My burdened child, and I will give you rest. Learn from Me—for I am humble and gentle—and in Me you will find rest for your weary soul. As a mother comforts her child, so will I comfort you.

In this life, there is a time for everything, a season for every activity under heaven. There is a time to be born and a time to die, a time to weep and a time to laugh, a time to mourn and a time to dance. Even though your loss is very painful, it should not come as a surprise to you. Because of the Evil One, even the best of your years are filled with pain and trouble.

But I am here to comfort you, for I am a God of compassion, and I comfort all My children in time of trouble. And I am here to heal you. I will restore you to your health and bring healing to your wounds. Even though you are walking through the valley of the shadow of death, don't be afraid, for I am with you. My rod and My staff will comfort you.

As you work through your pain, focus your eyes on Jesus, remembering that He was able to endure the pain of the cross because He looked forward to the joy ahead of Him. I will turn your wailing into dancing; I will remove your mourning clothes and clothe you with joy.

Your God of Comfort

from Matthew 11:28–29 NLT; Isaiah 66:13
Ecclesiastes 3:1–2, 4; 1 Peter 4:12; Psalm 90:10
2 Corinthians 1:3–4; Jeremiah 30:17
Psalm 23:4; Hebrews 12:2; Psalm 30:11

God's Word OF LOVE

ISAIAH 66:13
As a mother comforts her child, so will I comfort you.

MATTHEW 11:28–29 NLT
Come to me, all of you who are weary and
carry heavy burdens, and I will give you
rest. Take my yoke upon you. Let me teach
you, because I am humble and gentle, and
you will find rest for your souls.

ECCLESIASTES 3:1–2, 4
There is a time for everything, and a season for every
activity under heaven: a time to be born and a time to die,
a time to plant and a time to uproot, a time to weep and a
time to laugh, a time to mourn and a time to dance.

JEREMIAH 30:17
"I will restore you to health and heal your
wounds," declares the LORD.

HEBREWS 12:2
Let us fix our eyes on Jesus, the author
and perfecter of our faith, who for the
joy set before him endured the cross,
scorning its shame, and sat down at the
right hand of the throne of God.

PSALM 23:4
Even though I walk through
the valley of the shadow of
death, I will fear no evil, for
you are with me; your rod
and your staff, they comfort
me.

2 CORINTHIANS 1:3–4
Praise be to the God and Father of our Lord
Jesus Christ, the Father of compassion and
the God of all comfort, who comforts us in all
our troubles, so that we can comfort those in
any trouble with the comfort we ourselves
have received from God.

A LETTER TO *Heaven*

Dear Lord and Father,

The idea of "obedience" is not a very popular one. It goes against the grain of freedom and choice and independence—all the things our culture is built on. I know that You've told me that if I love You, I will keep Your commandments, but the idea of "submission" is a difficult concept for my self-reliant nature.

Accepting that Your way is the only way is contrary to the demand for "tolerance" in today's society—and I must admit, it's sometimes difficult for me to yield to You alone.

Teach me the value of obedience; soften my heart to Your lordship. When the thinking of the world threatens to dim my allegiance to You, please bring my heart in line with Your will. When my willful spirit rears its head, please remind me that You alone are sovereign, that You alone are Lord.

I confess to You, Lord, that there are certain things in me that I have not submitted to You. Certain relationships are strained and tense because I have not relinquished the pain of past offenses and because I have not admitted my own part in the offense. Certain obsessions eat away at my devotion to You. Fill me with such a love for You that obedience is my heart's desire.

Your Willful Child

A LETTER FROM *Heaven*

Dear Willful Child,

You must understand, My child, that My commands are for your good; they are not arbitrary limitations that I set on your life for the sake of displaying My power. My *love* for you is what is behind My commands. When you follow My teachings and obey My commands, you will find freedom, not restriction.

It's true that the prevailing thought of your culture is to accept any and all viewpoints of Me, but I Am Who I Am. I am the Alpha and the Omega, the First and the Last, the Beginning and the End. There is no other god besides Me. What people—whom *I* created—say about Me does not define Me. I am the LORD, and there is no other. In Me alone will your soul find rest and salvation. It is only in Me that you find hope. And it is through your obedience to Me and submission to My will that you demonstrate your love for Me.

This relationship between you and Me is based on love coming and going. I created you in love and have provided for you in love. What I ask in return is that you love Me. And love for Me can be defined only one way: that you obey My commands.

All of My law can be summed up in one word: *love*. Love Me with all your heart, soul, and mind, and love your neighbor as yourself.

Your One and Only God

from Psalm 119:45; Exodus 3:14–15
Revelation 1:8; 21:6; 22:13; Deuteronomy 4:39
Isaiah 45:6; Psalm 62:1, 5; 2 John 1:6
1 John 5:3; Matthew 22:37–40

God's Word OF LOVE

PSALM 119:45
I will walk about in freedom, for I have sought out your precepts.

DEUTERONOMY 4:39
Acknowledge and take to heart this day that the LORD is God in heaven above and on the earth below. There is no other.

EXODUS 3:14–15
I AM WHO I AM.... This is my name forever, the name by which I am to be remembered from generation to generation.

ISAIAH 45:6
I am the LORD, and there is no other.

PSALM 62:1, 5

My soul finds rest in God alone; my salvation
comes from him.... Find rest, O my soul, in God
alone; my hope comes from him.

REVELATION 22:13

I am the Alpha and the
Omega, the First and
the Last, the Beginning
and the End.

2 JOHN 1:6

And this is love: that
we walk in obedience
to his commands.

MATTHEW 22:37–40

Jesus replied: "'Love the Lord your God with all your heart
and with all your soul and with all your mind.' This is the
first and greatest commandment. And the second is like it:
'Love your neighbor as yourself.' All the Law and the
Prophets hang on these two commandments."

A LETTER TO *Heaven*

Dearest God,

Everything around me seems to be unraveling—everything! My family is making so many demands on me that I feel pulled apart like a wishbone. What *I* wish is that they would take care of their own needs for a little while—just long enough to let me catch my breath. My best friend is distracted by things in her own life. My family is sinking deeper and deeper into the hole of financial debt, and I don't see how our situation can improve.

Things aren't any better at work. My responsibilities are pressing me beyond my limits. I haven't worked an eight-hour day in months. If I don't stay late, I bring it home—and the work load keeps piling higher and higher. Work relationships that used to feel like family have become tense and competitive.

I don't know how my life got to this state, and I surely don't know how to make it right again. I've lost control. It's as if the demands and pressures around me are making my life's decisions, as if I don't have any say.

The pressure inside me is building. I'm afraid I'll either explode in anger or frustration or become completely immobilized. Can You help me, Lord? I'm going down fast.

Your Frenzied Child

A *Letter From* *Heaven*

Dear Frenzied Child,

I've seen the storm raging inside you for quite some time; I've just been waiting for you to get your eyes off yourself and your situation and look up to Me. Besides having too many demands and tensions in your life, you have too little of Me. This is your biggest problem of all. You are anxious and troubled about many things, when there is only one truly important thing, and that is to sit at My feet and learn of Me. You will find that if you seek Me first—putting Me above all else in your life—the rest of your life will find a new balance with Me at the center.

When I am at the center, you will begin to place the needs of others above your own—and that, too, will bring peace to your frenzied world. You'll be empowered to love even those who do not love you, to talk good about those who talk bad about you, and to pray for those who are unkind to you.

With Me at your center, you will be filled with My strength and thus will better be able to handle your responsibilities. I am your strength and your shield against the attacks upon your peace. I am a God who helps the fallen and lifts up those who are bent beneath their heavy load. Trust in Me, and I will bless you with inner peace.

Your God Who Calms Your Storms

from Luke 10:40–42; Matthew 6:25–34
Philippians 2:3–4; Matthew 5:44–45
Luke 6:27–28; 2 Samuel 22:33
Psalms 28:7; 29:11; 145:14 NLT

God's Word OF LOVE

PSALM 145:14 NLT
The LORD helps the fallen and lifts up those bent beneath their loads.

MATTHEW 6:33–34
But seek first his kingdom and his righteousness, and all these things will be given to you as well. Therefore do not worry about tomorrow, for tomorrow will worry about itself. Each day has enough trouble of its own.

2 SAMUEL 22:33
It is God who arms me with strength and makes my way perfect.

PHILIPPIANS 2:3–4
Do nothing out of selfish ambition or vain conceit, but in humility consider others better than yourselves. Each of you should look not only to your own interests, but also to the interests of others.

PSALM 29:11
The LORD gives
strength to his
people; the LORD
blesses his people
with peace.

LUKE 10:41–42
"Martha, Martha," the Lord answered, "you are worried
and upset about many things, but only one thing is
needed. Mary has chosen what is better, and it will not
be taken away from her."

PSALM 28:7
The LORD is my
strength and my
shield; my heart
trusts in him, and I
am helped. My heart
leaps for joy and I
will give thanks to
him in song.

MATTHEW 5:44–45
But I tell you: Love your enemies and pray for those who
persecute you, that you may be sons of your Father in
heaven. He causes his sun to rise on the evil and the good,
and sends rain on the righteous and the unrighteous.

A LETTER TO *Heaven*

Dear God of Protection,

I come to You today asking Your protection on my life and on the lives of those I love. My days, and the days of those close to me, are *filled* with potential danger and harm. Sometimes fear strangles my heart when I think about losing any of those I love, when I imagine the harm that could come to me or to them. For my children, my spouse, my friends, my extended family, I ask simply that You protect us.

When I am afraid, I put my trust in You. I look to You for protection. I hide beneath the shadow of Your wings. Please, Holy God, make Your face to shine upon us and be gracious to us. Only then will we be safe. I call upon You because I know You will answer. Show me Your unfailing love; save me with Your strength. Guard me as the apple of Your eye.

Protect me and mine from wicked people who would hurt us, from accidents that would incapacitate us, from sorrows and loss that would crush our hearts. Rise to Your feet, O Lord, and protect us from the evils and dangers of this world. It is You, O Lord, whom I trust. Please cover us with Your protective hand.

Trusting You

portions from Psalm 57:1 NLT; Numbers 6:25
Psalms 80:3; 17:6–8, 13

A LETTER FROM *Heaven*

Dear Trusting Child,

You have every reason to look to Me for protection, for I am your rock, your fortress, and your shield. In Me you will find safety and strength. When you are afraid, you can trust in Me, for I will not let you stumble and fall. I watch over you constantly—I never sleep. As a protective shade, I stand beside you. I keep you from all evil, preserving your life. I watch over you as you come and go—both now and forever.

In reality, mere mortals can do nothing that will harm you forever. Fearlessness is based not on freedom from physical harm or grief but on the knowledge that the things of this world are but temporary and that My hand of protection extends into eternity. Though you may have some trouble in this life, your heart can be free of fear because you know that My protection of you is ultimate, if not always immediate. So, you see, you don't need to fear those who would harm you, for they cannot touch your soul.

But even while you are in this life, I shield you with My wings and shelter you with My feathers. My faithful promises are your armor and protection. You need not fear the terrors of the night or the dangers of the day, for I have ordered My angels to protect you and watch over you wherever you go. I protect those who trust in My name.

Your Trustworthy God

from Psalms 18:2 NLT; 56:3–4 NLT; 121:3, 5, 7–8 NLT
Matthew 10:28; Psalm 91:4–6, 11, 14 NLT

God's Word OF LOVE

PSALM 18:2 NLT
The LORD is my rock, my fortress, and my savior; my God is my rock, in whom I find protection. He is my shield, the strength of my salvation, and my stronghold.

PSALM 57:1 NLT
I look to you for protection. I will hide beneath the shadow of your wings.

PSALM 17:6–8 NLT
I am praying to you because I know you will answer, O God. Bend down and listen as I pray. Show me your unfailing love in wonderful ways. You save with your strength those who seek refuge from their enemies. Guard me as the apple of your eye. Hide me in the shadow of your wings.

PSALM 80:3
Restore us, O God; make your face shine upon us, that we may be saved.

44

PSALM 91:4–5 NLT

He will shield you with his wings. He will shelter
you with his feathers. His faithful promises are your
armor and protection. Do not be afraid of the terrors
of the night, nor fear the dangers of the day.

PSALM 56:3–4 NLT

When I am afraid, I put my trust in you....
What can mere mortals do to me?

PSALM 91:11 NLT

He orders his angels to protect
you wherever you go.

PSALM 121:3, 5, 7–8 NLT

He will not let you stumble and fall; the one who watches
over you will not sleep.... The LORD stands beside you as
your protective shade. The LORD keeps you from all evil
and preserves your life. The LORD keeps watch over you
as you come and go, both now and forever.

A LETTER TO *Heaven*

Mysterious God,

You are so far above me, so powerful, so pure. Who can know Your thoughts? Who can understand Your ways? As the heavens are higher than the earth, so are Your ways higher than my ways and Your thoughts than mine. Your power and majesty are beyond my broadest reach. You adorn Yourself with glory and splendor; You clothe yourself in honor and majesty. Heaven is Your throne; the earth is Your footstool. You ride across the heavens on the clouds. Your power and majesty are beyond my comprehension.

Yet as powerful and marvelous as You are, You desire intimacy with me. This is beyond my scope of reason. It's too wonderful to be true. Yet I know it is. I, too, desire intimacy with You. It is You—Your thoughts, Your ways—that I seek. O God, You are my God; I seek You earnestly. My soul thirsts for You; even my body longs for You, as a person in a desert longs for water.

My heart says of You, "Seek His face!" Your face, O Lord, I will seek.

Earnestly Seeking You

portions from Isaiah 55:9; Job 40:10; Isaiah 66:1
Deuteronomy 33:26; Psalms 63:1; 27:8

A LETTER FROM *Heaven*

Dearest Child,

I love you for loving Me. I can assure you that because you seek Me, you will find Me. Though My thoughts are not your thoughts and My ways are not your ways, if you seek Me with all your heart and soul, you will assuredly find Me.

I am the one who formed the mountains and created the winds. I am He who turns dawn into darkness, who treads on the high places of the earth, yet I will reveal My thoughts to you. I tell you this: If you acknowledge Me and serve Me with wholehearted devotion and with a willing mind, if you seek Me with all your heart, I *will* be found by you. If you will call Me by name, if you will humble yourself before Me and pray, if you will seek My face and turn from your hurtful ways, then I will hear from heaven, I will forgive your sins and heal your land.

And now, as you seek Me, you must fix your eyes on My Son, Jesus, who is the beginning and ending of faith. For you He endured the cross, scorning its shame. He now sits at My right hand and intercedes before Me on your behalf.

Look always to Me and My strength; always seek My face. When you do this, your heart will be full of joy. I have never forsaken those who trust Me and truly seek after Me, and I will not forsake you.

Your Ever Near Father

from Proverbs 8:17; Isaiah 55:8; Deuteronomy 4:29
Amos 4:13; 1 Chronicles 28:9; 2 Chronicles 7:14
Hebrews 12:2; 7:25; 1 Chronicles 16:10–11; Psalm 9:10

God's Word OF LOVE

PSALM 63:1
O God, you are my God,
earnestly I seek you; my
soul thirsts for you, my
body longs for you, in a
dry and weary land
where there is no water.

PROVERBS 8:17
I love those who love me, and
those who seek me find me.

DEUTERONOMY 4:29
But if from there you seek the LORD
your God, you will find him if you look
for him with all your heart and with all
your soul.

PSALM 27:8
My heart says of you, "Seek his face!"
Your face, LORD, I will seek.

Amos 4:13

He who forms the mountains, creates
the wind, and reveals his thoughts to
man, he who turns dawn to darkness,
and treads the high places of the earth—
the Lord God Almighty is his name.

Psalm 9:10

Those who know your name will trust in
you, for you, Lord, have never forsaken
those who seek you.

1 Chronicles 16:11

Look to the Lord and his strength;
seek his face always.

1 Chronicles 28:9

Acknowledge the God of your father, and
serve him with wholehearted devotion and
with a willing mind, for the LORD searches
every heart and understands every motive
behind the thoughts. If you seek him, he
will be found by you; but if you forsake
him, he will reject you forever.

A LETTER TO *Heaven*

Dear Lord,

My heart is heavy, Lord, for I know I have greatly disappointed You. I've made so many promises to You that I haven't kept. I've made plans to do good that I haven't completed. I am so unworthy of Your love.

Thoughts of my failures consume me. I know people who need me to reach out to them, but I allow my own agenda and busyness to keep me from them. My mouth continues to get me in trouble. I think I have my tongue under control, and then someone pushes one of my buttons and I blow up. I resolve to spend a regular quiet time with You, but then I allow the responsibilities of my day to drain me of my best energy, and there's nothing left over for You. I don't know how many times I've determined to take control of my eating...but I never stick to my plan.

Feelings of guilt overwhelm me and render me even more powerless to live as I know You want me to. But even worse than the guilt is the fear that my failings have separated me from Your love.

I know my wrong actions and attitudes break Your heart. But I need to know, Lord, do You love me even though I so frequently disappoint You?

Your Disappointing Child

A LETTER FROM *Heaven*

Dear Child,

I know how weak you are, and yet I love you still. I love you like a father loves his children. I am tender and compassionate toward those who fear Me. Because I love you so much, I do not deal with you according to what you deserve. My unfailing love for you is as great as the height of the heavens is above the earth. I have removed even your rebellious acts as far away from Me as the east is from the west.

My unfailing love for you will never be shaken; My covenant of peace will not be removed. In truth, I *long* to be gracious to you. I rise to My feet to show you compassion. If you will wait on Me, you will see My hand upon your life.

You can know with assurance that as a child of Mine nothing can ever separate you from My love. My love for you is so powerful that neither death nor life, neither angels nor demons can separate Me from you. Your fears for today and your worries about tomorrow cannot come between us. Why, even the powers of hell can't keep My love from you. You couldn't go deep enough in the ocean or high enough in the sky to be separated from Me. My love for you endures forever—even when you disappoint Me.

Your Faithful Father

from Psalm 103:13–14 NLT; 10–12 NLT
Isaiah 54:10; 30:18; Romans 8:38–39 NLT
1 Chronicles 16:34

God's Word OF LOVE

PSALM 103:13–14 NLT
The LORD is like a father
to his children, tender
and compassionate to
those who fear him. For
he understands how
weak we are; he knows
we are only dust.

ISAIAH 30:18
Yet the LORD longs to be gracious to you; he rises to
show you compassion. For the LORD is a God of justice.
Blessed are all who wait for him!

PSALM 103:10–12 NLT
He has not punished us for all our sins, nor
does he deal with us as we deserve. For his
unfailing love toward those who fear him is as
great as the height of the heavens above the
earth. He has removed our rebellious acts as far
away from us as the east is from the west.

1 CHRONICLES 16:34
Give thanks to the LORD, for he is good; his love endures forever.

ROMANS 8:38–39 NLT
Nothing can ever separate us from his love. Death can't, and life can't. The angels can't, and the demons can't. Our fears for today, our worries about tomorrow, and even the powers of hell can't keep God's love away. Whether we are high above the sky or in the deepest ocean, nothing in all creation will ever be able to separate us from the love of God that is revealed in Christ Jesus our Lord.

PSALM 145:9 NLT
The Lord is good to everyone. He showers compassion on all his creation.

A LETTER TO *Heaven*

Dear God of Peace,

I've had a sense of uneasiness in my spirit for quite some time now. I can't really say when it began or what triggered it—but it's been growing, and its chaotic noise is so loud in my head that I can no longer ignore it.

This frustration, this lack of inner peace is not only affecting me; it's hurting all my relationships. I've been moody and temperamental; I've been unproductive and distracted. My spouse and children are getting the brunt of it, but even my coworkers are beginning to ask me if something is wrong.

I can't tell them, Lord, but *yes, something is very wrong!* I've lost the trusting peace that once governed my heart and frame of mind. Minor problems take on monumental proportions; concerns about the future haunt my present moments. I find myself fretting over other people's successes and my failures. I worry about what my coworkers, my family—even strangers—think of me and say about me when I'm not there. But worst of all, I feel uncertain of my relationship with You. I don't feel at peace with You. My failings loom like an impassable ocean between us.

I know this is not what You intend for me. Please restore Your peace to my heart and mind.

Your Tormented Child

A LETTER FROM *Heaven*

Dear Tormented Child,

I am the God of all grace; I am the one who called you into an eternal relationship with Christ, and I will restore you and make you strong, firm, and steadfast. I will bring health and healing to your troubled spirit so that you can once again enjoy abundant peace and security.

The cacophony you feel in your heart is there for two reasons: You've lost confidence in the peace that Jesus has created between you and Me, and you've allowed your fears to replace your trust in Me. Have you forgotten that My Son was pierced for your transgressions, that He was crushed for your iniquities? Do you not know that He has already taken your punishment on Himself, thus healing your wounds and granting you peace with Me? Remember that because of your faith in Jesus, you have perfect peace with Me.

Stir the embers of truth in your heart, and I will reignite a perfect peace in you, a peace that transcends all understanding, a peace that will guard your heart and mind. I am the Lord of peace, and as you trust in Me, I will give you peace at all times and in every way.

When you feel fretful and agitated, turn your thoughts to Me and wait patiently for Me. Do not fret over what other people do or say—fretting leads only to evil. Turn your face toward Mine, and let the light of My face shine upon you.

Your God of Peace

from 1 Peter 5:10; Jeremiah 33:6; Isaiah 53:5
Romans 5:1; Isaiah 26:3; Philippians 4:7
2 Thessalonians 3:16; Psalms 37:7–8; 4:6, 8

God's Word OF LOVE

1 PETER 5:10
And the God of all grace, who called you to his eternal glory in
Christ, after you have suffered a little while, will himself restore
you and make you strong, firm and steadfast.

ISAIAH 53:5
But he was pierced for our transgressions, he
was crushed for our iniquities; the punishment
that brought us peace was upon him, and by
his wounds we are healed.

ROMANS 5:1
Therefore, since we have been
justified through faith, we have
peace with God through our
Lord Jesus Christ.

2 THESSALONIANS 3:16
Now may the Lord of peace himself give you peace at
all times and in every way. The Lord be with all of you.

PSALM 4:6, 8
Let the light of your face shine upon us, O LORD. I will lie down and sleep in peace, for you alone, O LORD, make me dwell in safety.

PHILIPPIANS 4:7
And the peace of God, which transcends all understanding, will guard your hearts and your minds in Christ Jesus.

ISAIAH 26:3
You will keep in perfect peace him whose mind is steadfast, because he trusts in you.

PSALM 37:7–8
Be still before the LORD and wait patiently for him; do not fret when men succeed in their ways, when they carry out their wicked schemes. Refrain from anger and turn from wrath; do not fret—it leads only to evil.

A LETTER TO *Heaven*

Dear Father in Heaven,

Lately I've been overwhelmed with feelings of worthlessness. I feel alone and uncared for. These feelings have incapacitated me. I'm not being the parent I need to be to my children, my spouse is feeling neglected and unappreciated, I'm ignoring the few friends I have, and I'm totally unproductive at work.

When I look into the eyes of those around me, I find no evidence that I'm needed or wanted. I think I could disappear from the face of the earth and it wouldn't matter to a single soul. And why should they miss me? I'm not contributing anything to anyone.

My greatest fear—and this is going to sound ridiculous—but my greatest fear is that when I die, the only ones who will come to my funeral are those who feel obligated.

Where can I turn to find a sense of value? What can I do to actually *be* valuable? I'm feeling all alone out here and no good to anyone.

Your Worthless Child

A LETTER FROM *Heaven*

Dear Valued One,

You, My child, have value just because you are My child. Out of all the people on earth, you are one of My chosen ones; you are My treasured possession. I hear the cries of your heart, and I have listened. Your name is written in My scroll of remembrance as one who honors My name.

I do not love you because of what you accomplish; I love you because you are Mine. I love you with an everlasting love. I have drawn you to Myself with loving-kindness. You are valuable because *I* value you. That is reason enough. Though you feel that everyone else has abandoned you, know that I will never forsake you. Though your heart condemns you, you are not condemned. For I am greater than your heart. I am your God, and you are a sheep in My pasture and under My care.

Consider a little sparrow. Not one of them falls to the ground without My knowledge, and you are worth much more to Me than a sparrow. Even the very hairs of your head are numbered. I want you to cast all your anxiety on Me, because I *care* for you.

I am the God who made light to shine out of darkness, and I can make My light to shine in your heart. I am your refuge when you are troubled. Trust in Me, for I care for you.

Your God Who Cares

from Deuteronomy 14:1–2; Malachi 3:16
Deuteronomy 7:7–8; Jeremiah 31:3; Psalm 27:10
1 John 3:19–20; Psalm 95:7; Matthew 10:29–30
1 Peter 5:7; 2 Corinthians 4:6; Nahum 1:7

God's Word OF LOVE

DEUTERONOMY 14:1–2
You are the children of the LORD your God... Out of all the peoples on the face of the earth, the LORD has chosen you to be his treasured possession.

PSALM 27:10
Though my father and mother forsake me, the LORD will receive me.

NAHUM 1:7
The LORD is good, a refuge in times of trouble. He cares for those who trust in him.

JEREMIAH 31:3
The LORD appeared to us in the past, saying: "I have loved you with an everlasting love; I have drawn you with loving-kindness."

MALACHI 3:16
Then those who feared the LORD talked with each other, and the LORD listened and heard. A scroll of remembrance was written in his presence concerning those who feared the LORD and honored his name.

1 JOHN 3:19–20

This then is how...we set our hearts at rest in his presence whenever our hearts condemn us. For God is greater than our hearts, and he knows everything.

MATTHEW 10:29–30

Are not two sparrows sold for a penny? Yet not one of them will fall to the ground apart from the will of your Father. And even the very hairs of your head are all numbered.

2 CORINTHIANS 4:6

For God, who said, "Let light shine out of darkness," made his light shine in our hearts to give us the light of the knowledge of the glory of God in the face of Christ.

PSALM 95:7

For he is our God and we are the people of his pasture, the flock under his care.

DEUTERONOMY 7:7–8

The LORD did not set his affection on you and choose you because you were more numerous than other peoples.... But it was because the LORD loved you and kept the oath he swore to your forefathers.

A LETTER TO *Heaven*

Dear Lord,

I'm really struggling with something, and I hope You can help. There's this woman at church who is a real drain on my time and energy. If I allow myself to get in a conversation with her, she monopolizes all my time and keeps me from others who need me and whom I need. After all, don't I need encouragement too? I don't have the energy to invest in someone who is so "needy" and yet gives me nothing in return.

I know You want me to be a good "steward" of my time, and she seems a poor choice when there are other relationships and ministries that I really want to pursue. I keep thinking of the old adage: "God helps those who help themselves." If she would just make some efforts to better her life, maybe I'd be more inclined to help her.

But I must confess that something keeps haunting me, telling me that maybe my attitude isn't exactly what it needs to be, that maybe my priorities don't line up with Yours. That's why I've come to You. Help me to see this needy woman through Your eyes. Help my heart to be in tune with Yours. Teach me Your will.

Your Inquiring Steward

A LETTER FROM *Heaven*

Dear Misguided "Steward,"

I'm glad you came to Me for help, because you're right, your attitude isn't what it needs to be. There is no better way you could spend your time than in loving one of My children. In fact, when you share acts of kindness with those in need, you're actually doing those kindnesses to My Son, Jesus.

My admonition to you is that you live in harmony with this sister. That you not be proud, but rather that you willingly associate with her and with other people you consider to be of "low position." Watch your heart that it not be conceited.

All love comes from Me, and all who are born of Me live out My love. Because I have loved you, you are to love others. When you love others. I will live in you and My love will find full expression in you. I have given you the ultimate gift of love—My one and only Son. It is only through this gift that you have life at all. If I have given this great sacrifice, surely you can sacrifice your time for one of My needy children.

Consider the love and time you give to her—and others like her—to be a partial payment of the debt of love you owe. By loving her, you actually fulfill the whole intent of the law.

The God of the Needy

from Matthew 25:40; Romans 12:16
1 John 4:7–12; Romans 13:8

God's Word OF LOVE

MATTHEW 25:40
I tell you the truth, whatever you did for one of the least of these brothers of mine, you did for me.

1 JOHN 4:7–8
Dear friends, let us love one another, for love comes from God. Everyone who loves has been born of God and knows God. Whoever does not love does not know God, because God is love.

1 JOHN 4:12
No one has ever seen God; but if we love one another, God lives in us and his love is made complete in us.

1 JOHN 4:11
Dear friends, since God so loved us, we also ought to love one another.

ROMANS 12:16
Live in harmony with one another. Do not be
proud, but be willing to associate with people of
low position. Do not be conceited.

ROMANS 13:8
Let no debt remain outstanding, except the continuing
debt to love one another, for he who loves his fellowman
has fulfilled the law.

1 JOHN 4:9–10
This is how God showed his love
among us: He sent his one and
only Son into the world that we
might live through him. This is
love: not that we loved God, but
that he loved us and sent his Son
as an atoning sacrifice for our sins.

A LETTER TO *Heaven*

Dear God of Blessing,

I come to You, Lord, asking that You pour Your powerful blessings into my life. Along with Jabez of old, I ask that You bless me and enlarge my territory! Please be with me in all I do and keep me from trouble and pain.

I pray You will bless whatever I put my mind or hands to—whether it be at work, in my home, in my church or community. I ask that You bless my family with health, peace, and safety. Please bless me in my interactions with other people that I can be a tool in Your hand. Watch over me and bless me as I make decisions. I ask that You grant me the desires of my heart and make all my plans succeed. I petition You to multiply my efforts so that whatever I do will reap bountiful harvests. May Your unfailing love rest on me as I put my hope in You. May Your truth always protect me.

You have told me that if I will follow Your commands and walk in Your ways that You will bless me. I ask that You remember me and give me the blessings you've promised. I seek Your favor and ask that You—the Maker of heaven and earth—bless me and mine.

Seeking Your Blessings

portions from 1 Chronicles 4:10 NLT
Psalms 20:4; 33:22; 40:11; Deuteronomy 30:16
Psalm 115:12, 15

A LETTER FROM *Heaven*

Dear Beseeching Child,

I love you, My child, and long to bless you. I want to be gracious to you. You will be blessed if you wait on Me. You are the sheep of My pasture, and I am your God. My blessings bring wealth, and I add no trouble to it. I give strength to My people and bless them with peace.

I challenge you to test Me in My willingness to bless: Give to me a portion of all that is yours, then step back and watch what I will do. I will throw open the floodgates of heaven and pour out so much blessing that you will not have room for it. I *will* remember you and extend My favor to you so that you may enjoy the prosperity of My chosen ones. Keep your actions clean and your heart pure, and you will receive My bountiful blessing. I bless those who respect Me—whether they are great or small. I will give increase to both you and your children. Seek My face and see what I will do for you.

I will bless you and keep you; I will make My face to shine upon you and be gracious to you. I will turn My face toward you and give you peace.

Your God of Blessing

from Isaiah 30:18; Proverbs 10:22; Psalm 29:11
Malachi 3:10; Psalms 24:4-6; 106:4; 115:13-14
Numbers 6:24-26

God's Word OF LOVE

1 CHRONICLES 4:10 NLT
"Oh, that you would bless me and extend my lands! Please be with me in all that I do, and keep me from all trouble and pain!" And God granted him his request.

PSALM 20:4
May he give you the desire of your heart and make all your plans succeed.

PSALM 115:13–14
He will bless those who fear the LORD—small and great alike. May the LORD make you increase, both you and your children.

PSALM 33:22
May your unfailing love rest upon us, O LORD, even as we put our hope in you.

PSALM 115:12, 15
The LORD remembers us and will bless us.... May you be blessed by the LORD, the Maker of heaven and earth.

PROVERBS 10:22

The blessing of the LORD brings wealth, and he adds no trouble to it.

PSALM 24:4–6

He who has clean hands and a pure heart, who does not lift up his soul to an idol or swear by what is false. He will receive blessing from the LORD and vindication from God his Savior. Such is the generation of those who seek him, who seek your face, O God of Jacob.

MALACHI 3:10

"Bring the whole tithe into the storehouse, that there may be food in my house. Test me in this," says the LORD Almighty, "and see if I will not throw open the floodgates of heaven and pour out so much blessing that you will not have room enough for it."

NUMBERS 6:24–26

The LORD bless you and keep you; the LORD make his face shine upon you and be gracious to you; the LORD turn his face toward you and give you peace.

PSALM 106:4–5

Remember me, O LORD, when you show favor to your people, come to my aid when you save them, that I may enjoy the prosperity of your chosen ones, that I may share in the joy of your nation and join your inheritance in giving praise.

A LETTER TO *Heaven*

Dear God of Forgiveness,

I am so ashamed, Lord. I have failed You again. My guilt overwhelms me—it is a burden too heavy for me to bear. My soul festers with sorrow because of my foolish sin. My spirit is exhausted and completely crushed. Groaning comes from my anguished heart.

I come to You today, Lord, to confess my sin. I am so sorry for what I have done. Please don't hold Your tender mercies back from me. My only hope is in Your unfailing love and faithfulness.

I beg You, Father, because of Your great compassion, please blot out the stain of my sins. Purify me from my sin. Wash me clean from my guilt. If You wash me, I know I will be whiter than snow. I know that it is against You, and You alone, that I have sinned.

The temptation just crept up on me. I had good intentions in my spirit, but my flesh got the better of me. You know what I'm like, for You created me. I appeal to Your unwavering love and to the forgiveness You have provided through Your Son.

Can You forgive me once more?

Your Guilty Child

portions from Psalms 38:4–8, 18; 40:11; 51:1–2, 4, 7

A LETTER FROM *Heaven*

Dear Guilty Child,

Confessing your wrong is exactly what you needed to do. Because you acknowledged your sin and did not try to cover it up but freely confessed to Me, I will forgive you of your guilt. I am faithful and just and will cleanse you from all wrong. I ransom you from death and surround you with My love and tender mercy. I fill your life with good things.

It is only through the atoning sacrifice of Jesus that you can be forgiven. He personally bore your sins on His body on the cross so that you could be granted the forgiveness you long for. He was pierced for your transgressions; He was crushed for your wrongdoing. By His wounds, you are healed. Though He is My only Son, I made Him—who never did anything wrong—to bear your sin, so that you could be made right with Me.

There is much joy for you, now that your rebellion has been forgiven, for your sin has been put out of My sight. You can rejoice because I have wiped your record clean. You can shout for joy because your heart is pure! I have created in you a clean heart; I have renewed a right spirit within you. Now what I ask from you is that your heart remain broken and repentant—this is the kind of sacrifice I want.

Your Forgiving God

from Psalm 32:5; 1 John 1:9; Psalm 103:3–5 NLT
1 Peter 2:24 NLT; Isaiah 53:5; 2 Corinthians 5:21
Psalms 32:1–2, 11 NLT; 51:10, 17 NLT

God's Word OF LOVE

1 JOHN 1:9

If we confess our sins, he is faithful and just and will forgive us our sins and purify us from all unrighteousness.

2 CORINTHIANS 5:21

God made him who had no sin to be sin for us, so that in him we might become the righteousness of God.

1 PETER 2:24 NLT

He personally carried away our sins in his own body on the cross so we can be dead to sin and live for what is right. You have been healed by his wounds!

PSALM 103:3–5 NLT

He forgives all my sins and heals all my diseases. He ransoms me from death and surrounds me with love and tender mercies. He fills my life with good things.

PSALM 32:11 NLT
So rejoice in the LORD and be glad,
all you who obey him! Shout for joy,
all you whose hearts are pure!

PSALM 51:17 NLT
The sacrifice you want is a broken spirit. A broken
and repentant heart, O God, you will not despise.

PSALM 51:10 NLT
Create in me a clean heart, O God.
Renew a right spirit within me.

PSALM 32:1–2 NLT
Oh, what joy for those whose
rebellion is forgiven, whose sin
in put out of sight! Yes, what
joy for those whose record the
LORD has cleared of sin.

A LETTER TO *Heaven*

Dear God of Healing,

My heart is sad and encumbered with the burden of an unmended relationship. The eyes of my heart can see the injury, but I'm helpless to mend the tear. Past pain still haunts me; old mistakes reverberate in present consequences; wounds inflicted years ago still gape open. I come to You for healing, Lord, for I've made no progress on my own.

Some tell me that these old wounds can't be mended—that the damage is too deep, the injuries too severe. But I don't believe that, Lord. Your Word is filled with miraculous healings—not only of physical bodies but of nations and hearts. You are a God of restoration, of renewal, and refreshment. And now I come to You, on my knees, begging You to release Your miraculous healing into my life.

Please make a way to bridge the chasms that separate me from this person I love. Flood my heart and hers with Your healing love. My words are inadequate, my gestures empty. But Your love has the power to do the humanly impossible. Your love overpowers the chains of resentment and misunderstanding. Your unfailing love brings peace to turbulent souls.

Do it now, Lord; please release Your healing love.

Your Wounded Child

A LETTER FROM *Heaven*

Dear Wounded Child,

I hear you, child, and My heart goes out to you. I will restore your relationships and heal your wounds. I am a healer of broken hearts, and I allow My people to enjoy abundant peace and security.

When you call Me by name, when you humble yourself before Me and seek My face, then I will hear from heaven and bring healing to your life. If you will spend yourself on behalf of the hurting around you, your light will break forth like the dawn, and your healing will quickly appear. You will call out for My help, and I will say, "Here am I."

When I heal you, you will truly be healed; when I save you, you will be saved. When you are faint, I will be merciful to you; I will deliver you and save you because of My unfailing love.

I have seen your broken relationship, and I will heal you; I will guide you and restore comfort to you. If you will revere My name, the sun of righteousness will rise with healing in its wings, and you will go out and leap like a calf released from the stall. I will bring peace to those far and near; I will heal you and them.

Your God of Healing

from Jeremiah 30:17; 33:6; 2 Chronicles 7:14
Isaiah 58:8–10; Jeremiah 17:14; Psalm 6:2–4
Isaiah 57:18; Malachi 4:2; Isaiah 57:19

God's Word OF LOVE

ISAIAH 57:19
"Peace, peace, to those far and near," says the LORD. "And I will heal them."

2 CHRONICLES 7:14
If my people, who are called by my name, will humble themselves and pray and seek my face and turn from their wicked ways, then will I hear from heaven and will forgive their sin and will heal their land.

ISAIAH 57:18
I have seen his ways, but I will heal him; I will guide him and restore comfort to him.

JEREMIAH 33:6
Nevertheless, I will bring health and healing to it; I will heal my people and will let them enjoy abundant peace and security.

PSALM 6:2–4

Be merciful to me, LORD, for I am faint; O LORD, heal me, for my bones are in agony. My soul is in anguish. How long, O LORD, how long? Turn, O LORD, and deliver me; save me because of your unfailing love.

MALACHI 4:2

But for you who revere my name, the sun of righteousness will rise with healing in its wings. And you will go out and leap like calves released from the stall.

JEREMIAH 17:14

Heal me, O LORD, and I will be healed; save me and I will be saved, for you are the one I praise.

A LETTER TO *Heaven*

Dear God of Power,

My confidence has shriveled, and my heart is filled with defeat. It seems that everything I put my hand to fails.

There have been times in my life when I felt I could accomplish anything, when whatever I tried to do, I did—and did it well. When I had a decision to make, I'd weigh my options and quickly come to a wise conclusion. When I invested myself in a project, I reaped success; I received praises from those who witnessed my victories.

But all that is gone now. I'm afraid to make decisions; I'm fearful of new situations. Even jobs and relationships I've succeeded in for years I now face with dread and uncertainty. And I can see my lack of self-confidence reflected in the faces of others. Those who used to trust my insight and direction now doubt everything I say and challenge any idea I present.

I need Your help to get out of this slump. Please grant me success; please give me wisdom in decision making; please fill me with confidence once again.

Your Failing Child

A LETTER FROM *Heaven*

Dear Failing Child,

You *can* be filled with confidence again, but you must first understand the source of true confidence. You shouldn't be surprised that you have met with failure and incompetence, for you are not competent in yourself. Your confidence and your competence come only from your relationship with Me.

I have begun a good work in you, and I will carry it to completion. You can say with unwavering confidence, "The Lord is my helper; I will not be afraid. What can mere mortals do to me?" You *will* be blessed if you put your confidence and trust in Me—not in yourself. (You will be like a tree planted along a riverbank, with roots that reach deep into the water. Such trees are not bothered by the heat or worried by long months of drought. Their leaves stay green, and they go right on producing delicious fruit.)

When *I* am your confidence, you don't need to fear disaster or ruin, for I will keep your foot from entanglement. As you put your trust in Me, My unfailing love will surround you. If you will live an upright life, you will be filled with peace, quietness, and confidence—forever.

Your God of Confidence

from 2 Corinthians 3:4–5; Philippians 1:6
Hebrews 13:6; Jeremiah 17:7–8 NLT; Proverbs 3:25–26
Psalm 32:10; Isaiah 32:17

God's Word OF LOVE

HEBREWS 13:6
So we say with confidence, "The Lord is my helper;
I will not be afraid. What can man do to me?"

2 CORINTHIANS 3:4–5
Such confidence as this
is ours through Christ
before God. Not that we
are competent in
ourselves to claim
anything for ourselves,
but our competence
comes from God.

PROVERBS 3:25–26
Have no fear of sudden
disaster or of the ruin
that overtakes the
wicked, for the LORD will
be your confidence and
will keep your foot from
being snared.

PHILIPPIANS 1:6
[Be] confident of this, that he who began a good
work in you will carry it on to completion until
the day of Christ Jesus.

PSALM 32:10
The LORD's unfailing love surrounds
the man who trusts in him.

ISAIAH 32:17
The fruit of righteousness will be
peace; the effect of righteousness will
be quietness and confidence forever.

JEREMIAH 17:7-8 NLT
Blessed are those who trust in the LORD and
have made the LORD their hope and confidence.
They are like trees planted along a riverbank,
with roots that reach deep into the water. Such
trees are not bothered by the heat or worried by
long months of drought. Their leaves stay green,
and they go right on producing delicious fruit.

A LETTER TO *Heaven*

Most Wonderful God,

On this day, my heart is overflowing with thanks for Your wonderful love. I am so overjoyed that I want to sing of Your great love forever. I want to make Your faithfulness known to all generations. I hereby declare to all that Your love stands forever firm, that Your faithfulness has been established in heaven itself. Your love is so dependable that I can trust You to love me in all situations and at all times. You satisfy me in the morning with Your unfailing love, so much so that I am filled with song and joy all my days.

I thank You that You are so patient with me, so slow to anger. I praise You for Your abounding love and Your forgiving nature. I thank You that You are a good and kind God and that You use Your omnipotent power to do us good and not harm. Thank You for loving me so much that You gave Your one and only Son to die in my place. I praise You for adopting me as Your child, for taking me into Your heart.

You are a great and awesome God. I thank You for keeping Your covenant of love with me as I obey Your commands.

Your Grateful Child

portions from Psalms 89:1–2; 52:8; 90:14
Numbers 14:18; 1 Chronicles 16:34
John 3:16; Nehemiah 1:5

A LETTER FROM *Heaven*

Dear Grateful Child,

It is good to give thanks to Me, for My love for you endures forever. Don't ever forget that I am a faithful God. I keep My covenant of love to a thousand generations of those who love Me and keep My commands. I am a gracious and compassionate God; you can count on Me not to desert you. I will save you in My unfailing love; I turn My face to you and let it shine on you. I hear your prayers and will not reject them, nor will I withhold My love from you.

My love for you is higher than the heavens, and My faithfulness reaches to the skies. I delight in you because you honor Me and put your hope in My unfailing love.

Before I created the world, I chose you to be My own. I predestined you to be adopted as My child, and now I love you as a father loves his child. I also love you as a husband loves his wife. You will be My wife forever; I will show you righteousness and justice, unfailing love and compassion. I will be faithful to you and make you Mine.

I love you with an everlasting love.

Your God of Love

from 1 Chronicles 16:34; Deuteronomy 7:9
Nehemiah 9:17; Psalms 31:16; 66:20; 108:4; 147:11
Ephesians 1:4–5; Hosea 2:19–20 NLT; Jeremiah 31:3

 *God's Word* OF LOVE

PSALM 52:8
I trust in God's unfailing love for ever
and ever.

PSALM 31:16
Let your face shine on
your servant; save me in
your unfailing love.

1 CHRONICLES 16:34
Give thanks to the LORD, for he is good; his love
endures forever.

PSALM 89:1–2
I will sing of the LORD's great love forever;
with my mouth I will make your faithfulness
known through all generations. I will declare
that your love stands firm forever, that you
established your faithfulness in heaven itself.

NEHEMIAH 1:5
God of heaven, the great and awesome
God, who keeps his covenant of love
with those who love him and obey
his commands.

NEHEMIAH 9:17
You are a forgiving God, gracious and compassionate, slow to anger and abounding in love. Therefore you did not desert them.

PSALM 147:11
The LORD delights in those who fear him, who put their hope in his unfailing love.

EPHESIANS 1:4–5
For he chose us in him before the creation of the world to be holy and blameless in his sight. In love he predestined us to be adopted as his sons through Jesus Christ, in accordance with his pleasure and will.

HOSEA 2:19–20 NLT
I will make you my wife forever, showing you righteousness and justice, unfailing love and compassion. I will be faithful to you and make you mine.

PSALM 108:4
For great is your love, higher than the heavens; your faithfulness reaches to the skies.

If you enjoyed this book, you'll also enjoy…

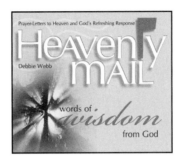

Heavenly Mail:
Words of Wisdom from God
ISBN: *1-58229-233-7*

Heavenly Mail:
Words of Encouragement from God
ISBN: *1-58229-169-1*

Heavenly Mail:
Words of Promise from God
ISBN: *1-58229-168-3*

Someone you know needs a hug today...

Hugs for Grandma
ISBN: *1-58229-154-3*

Hugs for New Moms
ISBN: *1-58229-223-X*

Hugs for Girlfriends
ISBN: *1-58229-224-8*

Other great Hugs™ books

Hugs for Teens
ISBN: *1-58229-213-2*

Hugs for Daughters
ISBN: *1-58229-214-0*

Hugs for Grads
ISBN: *1-58229-155-1*

Hugs for Friends
ISBN: *1-58229-006-7*

Hugs for Sisters
ISBN: *1-58229-095-4*

Hugs for Women
ISBN: *1-878990-81-0*

Hugs for Those in Love
ISBN: *1-58229-097-0*

Hugs for Mom
ISBN: *1-878990-69-1*

Hugs for Dad
ISBN: *1-878990-70-5*

Hugs for Teachers
ISBN: *1-58229-007-5*

Hugs for the Holidays
ISBN: *1-878990-74-8*

Hugs for Grandparents
ISBN: *1-878990-80-2*

Hugs for Kids
ISBN: *1-58229-096-2*

Hugs for the Hurting
ISBN: *1-878990-68-3*

**Hugs to Encourage
and Inspire**
ISBN: *1-878990-67-5*

**Hugs from Heaven—
Celebrating Friendship**
ISBN: *1-58229-130-6*

**Hugs from Heaven—
The Christmas Story**
ISBN: *1-58229-082-2*

**Hugs from Heaven—
On Angel Wings**
ISBN: *1-878990-90-X*

**Hugs from Heaven—
Embraced by the Savior**
ISBN: *1-878990-91-8*

**Hugs from Heaven—
Portraits of a
Woman's Faith**
ISBN: *1-58229-129-2*

...it may even be you!

Heartlifters® books to make the heart soar…

Heart-shaped, foldout pages reveal personalized, paraphrased Scripture.

Heartlifters for Women
ISBN: *1-58229-073-3*

Other great Heartlifters® books

Heartlifters for Teachers
ISBN: *1-58229-158-6*

Heartlifters for Sisters
ISBN: *1-58229-203-5*

Heartlifters for the Hurting
ISBN: *1-58229-202-7*

Heartlifters for Sisters
ISBN: *1-58229-203-5*

**Heartlifters for
the Young at Heart**
ISBN: *1-58229-157-8*

Heartlifters for Friends
ISBN: *1-58229-100-4*

Heartlifters for Hope and Joy
ISBN: *1-58229-074-1*

Heartlifters for Mom
ISBN: *1-58229-101-2*